"*Carnets* is not a notebook in any conventional sense. Rather, this collection of aphorisms is a great firefly filled with sparks, exploding and scattering in forever new and unexpected perceptions and revelations. This is a book that should be kept on hand for when the world appears dull or depressing. Its incisive, sometimes ruthless, unnerving, stimulating and unpredictable insights will always challenge and enlighten."

   —ANDREW TAYLOR, Emeritus Professor of Creative Humanities,
     Edith Cowan University, Australia

"With these glimpses, glances, snatches, squints, blinks, wells, catches, roots, tastes, and pinpricks, Kevin Hart delivers the cutting edge of more than fifty years of poetry (1974–2025). A unified existence that, from philosophy to literature and Christianity, reveals a renewed and creative way of seeing the world."

   —EMMANUEL FALQUE, Honorary Dean of the Faculty of Philosophy,
     Catholic University of Paris

"A carnet is a notebook—one thinks of Levinas and Camus—but it is also a customs permit for crossing a frontier. Each of Kevin Hart's marvelous aphorisms, gnomic and piquant, witty and lyrical, offers the wisdom of provocation. 'The bigger the truth, the fewer the words,' he writes. Then, as if to prove it: 'Loss is the boss.' There are fine insights into poetry: 'To write one line, one must forget many books.' And faith: 'God calls us home where we have never been.' And dailiness: 'Salt life with death—just enough.' *Carnets* is the work of fifty years, and I imagine it will last as long as people read."

   —DAVID MASON, author of *The Sound: New and Selected Poems*

"In this series of one-sentence poems that shift between question, declaration, lyric and aphorism, Kevin Hart brings a weight of experience, curiosity and clarity to the life of the body embedded in the life of the spirit. As they move between the quotidian and the visionary, these tiny, durable poems flash with insight and astonishment."

   —TOBY MARTINEZ DE LAS RIVAS, author of *Floodmeadow*

"At once evocative and elusive, Hart's poetic aphorisms pull you deeper into earthly experience in all its fleshy phenomenality only to push you over the edge into a bottomless well of bracing ideas. Savor one a day as 'espresso for the soul' and by the time you get to the end you'll want to start over with new eyes for the patterns they weave. 'Some trees carve their names in our heart': so too will some of the stunning one-liners in Hart's *Carnets*."

—KATE RIGBY, author of *Meditations on Creation in an Era of Extinction*

"Hart distills entire worlds in a mere handful of words. Lurking in these ecstatic fragments is a lifetime's worth of beauty and pain, wisdom and folly, body and spirit, gravity and levity. In *Carnets*, we see how Hart can be trusted with very little and so can also be trusted with much."

—JAYA SAVIGE, author of *Change Machine*

"Kevin Hart's *Carnets* reduces the aphoristic to its purest, most concentrated essence. The result is a series of intense, momentary pleasures, singular in their momentary realization, universal in their inexhaustible variety."

—JOHN KOETHE, Distinguished Professor of Philosophy Emeritus, The University of Wisconsin-Milwaukee

CARNETS

THE POIEMA POETRY SERIES

Poems are windows into worlds; windows into beauty, goodness, and truth; windows into understandings that won't twist themselves into tidy dogmatic statements; windows into experiences. We can do more than merely peer into such windows; with a little effort we can fling open the casements, and leap over the sills into the heart of these worlds. We are also led into familiar places of hurt, confusion, and disappointment, but we arrive in the poet's company. Poetry is a partnership between poet and reader, seeking together to gain something of value—to get at something important.

Ephesians 2:10 says, "We are God's workmanship . . ." *poiema* in Greek— the thing that has been made, the masterpiece, the poem. The Poiema Poetry Series presents the work of gifted poets who take Christian faith seriously, and demonstrate in whose image we have been made through their creativity and craftsmanship.

These poets are recent participants in the ancient tradition of David, Asaph, Isaiah, and John the Revelator. The thread can be followed through the centuries—through the diverse poetic visions of Dante, Bernard of Clairvaux, Donne, Herbert, Milton, Hopkins, Eliot, R. S. Thomas, and Denise Levertov—down to the poet whose work is in your hand. With the selection of this volume you are entering this enduring tradition, and as a reader contributing to it.

—D.S. Martin
Series Editor

CARNETS

KEVIN HART

CASCADE *Books* • Eugene, Oregon

CARNETS

Poiema Poetry Series

Cascade Books
An Imprint of Wipf and Stock Publishers
199 W. 8th Ave., Suite 3
Eugene, OR 97401

www.wipfandstock.com

PAPERBACK ISBN: 979-8-3852-5355-5
HARDCOVER ISBN: 979-8-3852-5356-2
EBOOK ISBN: 979-8-3852-5357-9

Cataloguing-in-Publication data:

Names: Hart, Kevin.

Title: Carnets / Kevin Hart.

Description: Eugene, OR: Cascade Books, 2025 | Series: Poiema Poetry Series

Identifiers: ISBN 979-8-3852-5355-5 (paperback) | ISBN 979-8-3852-5356-2 (hardcover) | ISBN 979-8-3852-5357-9 (ebook)

Subjects: LCSH: Poetry. | Christian poetry.

Classification: PN1010 H37 2025 (paperback) | PN1010 (ebook)

08/26/25

for Sashanna

Contents

.

Acknowledgments

SOME PASSAGES OF CARNETS have appeared in *Arena*, *Ekstasis*, and *Quadrant*. My thanks to all editors. I would also like to acknowledge the encouragement by various readers who have responded to this book in one or more of its many versions over the years, especially Michael Edwards, Gavin Flood, Phil Gates, John Koethe, Murray Littlejohn, Toby Martinez de las rivas, David Mason, Thomas Pfau, James Richardson, Stephanie Rumpza, and my wife, Sashanna Hart. I am thankful to Don Martin for his advice on the manuscript.

HORIZONS

1.

Poems unpeel the moment's skin.

2.

I sing my spirit into flesh.

3.

Only the good overflows, evil seeks channels.

4.

The bird's wings are no burden.

5.

Exhaust doubt before it exhausts you.

6.

If I didn't want her, I wouldn't want my flesh.

7.

The Bible is a beehive: honey and stings.

8.

Another day: the pilgrim starts anew; the grim pill pushes on.

9.

Tears taste of the oceans we must cross.

10.

Revere your enemies: they teach you things no friend would dare.

11.

What is lost nourishes us too.

12.

Death never raises his eyebrows.

13.

The gods don't live in mirrors.

14.

Salt life with death — just enough.

15.

Philosophy: running a comb through unruly ideas.

16.

The knife cherishes its glint.

17.

Ivy riots on the doorframe: Summer.

18.

Go to the desert, return with older eyes.

19.

My shadow goes barefoot on wet grass.

20.

Some sentences push us over the border of experience.

21.

The best poems are still thinking.

22.

We must waste time so as not to be afraid of it.

23.

No man comes home from war, but war sometimes comes home in a man.

24.

A Calvinist hope: The bleak shall inherit the earth.

25.

Fear arms the self.

26.

Another logic leapfrogs through the day.

27.

Poets hear the mating call of words.

28.

Fingertips are hedonists.

29.

The heart's a cat: all purrs and claws.

30.

I peel away your face to see your face.

31.

Flesh is a flower.

32.

The "I": a door, a corridor; and then?

33.

The heart must grow a backbone.

34.

There are thoughts that prefer to stay in back rooms.

35.

The most exacting inquisitor lives within.

36.

"I think therefore I am." — So, most people don't exist?

37.

When an answer crouches in a question — kill it.

38.

The apple remembers too much.

39.

The world is death; and still we buy its wares.

40.

At night stones feed on darkness.

41.

Marriage: four eyes and a bigger world to see.

42.

A rainstorm gobbles up the day.

43.

Vultures circle the phoenix's nest.

44.

Efforts to be great often blind us to greatness itself.

45.

Temptation always speaks in one's own voice.

46.

The stairs to heaven usually go by way of the basement.

47.

Don't rub your hands, fly, you haven't won yet!

48.

Dreams are tangled sleep.

49.

Some places are too big for justice, others too small.

50.

Don't speak just to the mirror: the horizon also wants to hear.

GLIMPSES

1.

Clocks are good at death, not life.

2.

Wisdom's enemies never see her naked.

3.

Ideology is squinting through the lens of politics.

4.

Method climbs no hills.

5.

Inside the heart, beasts tense to leap.

6.

Houses, too, have pores: doors and windows.

7.

Death makes more metaphysicians than Being ever does.

8.

Glance at evil by all means, but gaze upon the good.

9.

Poetry is the eye of the needle and the point of the needle.

10.

Blackberries teach us that the dark is sweet.

11.

A sun parakeet is a flying palette.

12.

Hatred sets your name in bold; joy takes your name away.

13.

Sin can be forgiven, guilt can't.

14.

We are eternal, even in this life, if we want to be.

15.

Time dies too; it's sweet revenge.

16.

Dipping my hand, I lift the lake's hem . . .

17.

We aim for truth and settle for justice.

18.

The abyss is an ocean; it laps at our feet.

19.

For us, the saints are barbed wire before they're love.

20.

Starve intelligence once in a while so that it doesn't become cleverness.

21.

There's no point crying over spilt religion.

22.

You cannot walk through a mirror, but a mirror can walk through you.

23.

The knots in wood are aphorisms.

24.

Grains of time stick to flesh.

25.

"Begin again," the ocean sighs.

26.

What idiot hired you, carpenter bee?

27.

One doesn't need a capacity for self-criticism if one has a child.

28.

That sudden twinge: it's only eternity trying to find a way in.

29.

Loaded with darkness, the freight train prays all night long.

30.

My gaze weeds the world.

31.

The smell of fresh celery: and I feel clean.

32.

Knives know we're wicked; they wink at us.

33.

To write is to make yourself a spirit before death.

34.

They had to cover the mirror; it had sprung a leak.

35.

The truth at last! His underwear on a clothesline!

36.

The eyelid is the most powerful part of the body.

37.

A poem always sets a world at risk.

38.

Questions like mosquitoes, questions like hornets . . .

39.

Poetry is the soil and the blossom

40.

We pray in part to make God manifest to ourselves.

41.

Snow puts the world in brackets.

42.

God calls us home where we have never been.

43.

Knives, also, dream of blossoming.

44.

Wise people fool around; it stops them from becoming fools.

45.

Poems caress the world so as to feel its mystery.

46.

How helpless her hands as evening comes . . .

47.

Both eyes for questions, one eye for answers, alas.

48.

The temptations of youth turn on the desire for life; those of age twist around the fear of death.

49.

The room's heaviest furniture is what has happened here.

50.

Her laughter is a carnation.

GLANCES

1.

Some thoughts sleep like cats, then pounce.

2.

Keep a room free for too long and death will move in.

3.

For sale at Low Church Ecclesiastical Supplies: incense alarms.

4.

A new notebook goes straight to one's head.

5.

Each room is a thousand rooms.

6.

Divorce is bitter honey.

7.

Summer: her eyelashes filled with salt and sleep.

8.

A whole world fits into a cat's jaws.

9.

Surely an ancient spider invented the umbrella.

10.

My morning coffee says: You're a mug.

11.

When you go to bed at night death creeps in beside you.

12.

A pleasure of summer is showing the body; a pleasure of winter is hiding it.

13.

Life: a hummingbird by goldenrod.

14.

Each morning we put on our manacles and admire ourselves in a mirror.

15.

Some words cast shadows on other words.

16.

Time blooms only when she enters my room.

17.

In sickness only pain is lucid.

18.

Clocks and mirrors understand each other all too well.

19.

We like to have God in the past and future, not in the present.

20.

Celibates are sometimes wise, bachelors never.

21.

Some rooms might be naked; none is ever empty.

22.

The silk begins to fray just by itself.

23.

God asks next to nothing of us because we are, in the end, next to nothing.

24.

Books are arrows; minds are bows.

25.

Who reads Death's palm?

26.

We shelter big memories in little things.

27.

Poor words become rich in poems.

28.

In the end, our childhoods eat us whole.

29.

Each poem completes a world.

30.

Truth always bears a few wounds.

31.

We seek refuge in the empty spaces between our thoughts.

32.

My name sleeps for twenty-three hours a day.

33.

Truth does not bend, but over the centuries it sways.

34.

Our best selves are perfect forgeries.

35.

The dogwood's blossoms are its prayer.

36.

Humid days: the whole summer is glued together.

37.

Time, also, has weeds.

38.

Some questions stick out their tongues at us.

39.

Even silence gets dirty.

40.

The magnolias sway to Muddy Waters, not the breeze.

41.

Between a mystery and a mystification — an abyss.

42.

In the end, our teachers disappoint us: it may be their greatest lesson.

43.

It's terrible to think that God prays to me.

44.

Even torturers go to the dentist.

45.

She bares her soul by walking barefoot.

46.

Poems grow from scraps; yet they look down on us.

47.

Books are building blocks.

48.

God needed only two bits of wood to save us.

49.

We wander in darkness, and darkness wanders in us.

50.

The bigger the truth, the fewer the words.

SNATCHES

1.

Open the mirror but be careful what you take from it.

2.

Early successes eventually become a species of failure.

3.

The darker the evenings, the deeper the thoughts.

4.

Befriend silence before you live in fear of it.

5.

We pray worse than we write.

6.

I open a window, but anger remains in the room.

7.

Freedom limps.

8.

Age begins when one thinks, "It's too late to . . ."

9.

The truth in champagne is mostly burst bubbles.

10.

The bigger the story, the more the devil falters.

11.

Little truths have the sharpest teeth.

12.

One tends a garden as one trains a choir.

13.

Prose is the freeway, poetry the rumble strip.

14.

In airplanes we feel like the eggs of hungry hens.

15.

Philosophy helps theology to be itself.

16.

A steady diet of politics starves the truth.

17.

The haystack is also down my back.

18.

Long thoughts cool us down.

19.

In winter we check sunlight to see if it's still there.

20.

Family photographs are the sharpest needles.

21.

We hope we age like the night, not the day.

22.

Weak thoughts hide life.

23.

Americans confuse sentiment with virtue.

24.

The whole night whispers about the owl.

25.

Trees are always listening.

26.

Ideas have grace notes too.

27.

Your library is your undersong.

28.

Enjoy your moment, dandelions!

29.

We pay for our place on the planet by leaving it.

30.

Shadows seldom venture very far.

31.

Ink is semen that sometimes meets an invisible egg.

32.

Young trees in Spring are natural flirts.

33.

Some desks are battle fields; others, temples.

34.

Loss is the boss.

35.

We can never go deep enough into the night.

36.

Clocks never cry.

37.

Some men keep distance in their hearts.

38.

A breath of sunlight, the rain's caesura.

39.

If you swallow a truth, you may well choke on it.

40.

Some poems are songs; others, theorems.

41.

Death's shadow keeps getting shorter.

42.

God has many lovers but he's always free for a date.

43.

Enter yourself (but take a deep breath first).

44.

In summer, days stray from the pack.

45.

If God sees our whole lives at once, we are millipedes.

46.

Early winter: petals of snow.

47.

A genius unfolds the creases in reality.

48.

Time holds us between thumb and forefinger.

49.

When we are in love, there is no better love.

50.

Solitude is sweet when you know it won't last.

SQUINTS

1.

The deaths of others measure our lives.

2.

On bad days we are complex equations that equal zero.

3.

Few marveled at moonlight in Sparta or Rome.

4.

Some lives are like rivers; others, lakes.

5.

Sometimes we wait lightly, sometimes hard.

6.

Each day begins by groping for its vanishing points.

7.

Infinity is despair; eternity, joy.

8.

I am left-handed: my hand was corrected, I was not.

9.

Some sorrows take root even in one's bones.

10.

The void, too, has angels: we hear their messages constantly.

11.

Some people stand in corners even when no corner is in sight.

12.

If they could, the stars would pray to us.

13.

The imagination is a beloved tyrant.

14.

We live too long and not enough.

15.

Good letters are deep breaths.

16.

No intelligibility without goodness.

17.

We spend life giving evidence against ourselves to an unknown judge.

18.

Each day has its own strangeness.

19.

Haloes cast shadows.

20.

High art does not disdain low emotions.

21.

True thought is praise.

22.

Light is luxury.

23.

When we are young, ideas affect us like passionate kisses.

24.

Young children are the staunchest conservatives.

25.

The crack in my plate leads straight to my childhood home.

26.

Prayer is the earnest money of eternal life.

27.

Ask yourself: How many borders run through me?

28.

Dreams trip up time.

29.

In hell one cannot forget oneself; that is the punishment.

30.

Light also blossoms in the apple tree.

31.

Life's currency is worn down pain.

32.

When learning the grammar of love, we begin with the subjunctive.

33.

The intellect has many doors, mostly locked.

34.

We admire roses but step on fallen petals.

35.

You can close doors on the living, not the dead.

36.

Visit the genius but live with the wise.

37.

Philosophy at dawn is a tonic, but by evening one has a hangover.

38.

Spiritual experience is seldom conscious: so we deny it.

39.

Even the closest things are far away.

40.

A grown mayfly lives a whole day — more than we do.

41.

Life: inflection, deflection, reflection.

42.

Meanings swarm in the room (and darker meanings in the closet).

43.

Don't dance on someone's grave; the ground nearby is smoother.

44.

Work hides and reveals life at exactly the same time.

45.

Love says "I," hoping it's heard as "we."

46.

When writing one must be alone (and never alone).

47.

Religion raises us above ourselves; art raises us higher, but only momentarily.

48.

Roadkill all along the abandoned road ...

49.

Some truths smell of bleach.

50.

Don't trust the mountain, trust the horizon.

BLINKS

1.

A circle of lamplight on the dark desk: tomorrow.

2.

Ideas are eels.

3.

Better to nurse your beer than your grudge.

4.

The truth is in the dance.

5.

A fall, too, is part of the dance.

6.

Today is rooted in my birth; tomorrow, in my death.

7.

The opal's bazaar.

8.

We're barely here and yet we stamp our feet.

9.

Life: a tune played on a piano — or, for some, a pianola

10.

Bells bruise the air.

11.

Some philosophers pass on the grilled salmon but gladly take the pepper.

12.

Worlds resist translation.

13.

Every crown has thorns.

14.

Late summer afternoon: rancid light.

15.

Bad thoughts swarm, good ones shine.

16.

At night even windows ask us to consider ourselves.

17.

A poem's kiss is worth a library.

18.

The world outgrows the names we give to it.

19.

Pear trees are swaying in their petticoats.

20.

New house: fresh sunlight on the stairs.

21.

If you walk in darkness, wear squeaky shoes.

22.

For some, books are jurors; for others, judges.

23.

Life consists of lessons in how to punctuate time.

24.

Australia is proof that tomorrow exists.

25.

The knife, too, is lucid.

26.

I do not own my breath.

27.

What we cannot name frightens us the most.

28.

What artwork indicts you? And for what?

29.

The more glass there is, the bigger the bill.

30.

Old money sleeps the soundest.

31.

Dry summer days: songs with dust for words.

32.

Christ's peace breaks us into pieces.

33.

We contemplate the future and meditate on the past.

34.

We spend life scrubbing away our shadows on the floor.

35.

Stone, soil, sun: we come — and it's a world!

36.

Love is gossamer that keeps us warm.

37.

Winter comes in morse code.

38.

A fat wind flounces through the door.

39.

Parmenides clearly never moved house.

40.

Politicians say all men are equal; historians and novelists, never.

41.

A philosophical question always brings all its family along.

42.

Once you believe in God, everything praises him.

43.

If you put the past down, it won't be there when you return.

44.

Metaphysics has a way of pushing in front of physics.

45.

When not a trinity, poetry, philosophy and music hate each other.

46.

We forget the sharp as well as the blunt.

47.

We long for balance only when tottering.

48.

Each profession looks down upon the others.

49.

Is death a blank or a blink?

50.

There's little to say and we spend life not saying it.

WELLS

1.

As we age we quietly tuck in the corners of our lives.

2.

Some art gluts us with truth.

3.

We pass from likeness to likeness, not from god to God.

4.

Lives have a beginning, a muddle, and an end.

5.

Empty bookshelves are more voracious than empty stomachs.

6.

Love without friendship is moonlight.

7.

Sleep is a luxury hotel in which we prefer the basement room.

8.

Like wind chimes, some books tell us when a change comes through.

9.

When tuning up, the orchestra is a menagerie.

10.

Modernity looks over your shoulder while talking with you.

11.

Every garden reminds us of what we have lost.

12.

An arrow remembers fingertips while lunging for the heart.

13.

In time the lines of the hand become the lines of the face.

14.

Reading brings reality up close.

15.

Good questions have empty hands.

16.

Absent a love for the world, criticism becomes hatred of it.

17.

The heart is a specialist that should be a generalist.

18.

There's always time for pain.

19.

Rhythm always allows plenty of space for falsehoods.

20.

Perception is also self-oblivion.

21.

Be honest, do you wish to teach the living or the dead?

22.

Life keeps misplacing us, waiting for death to find us.

23.

The rain becomes bolder once we go to bed.

24.

We remember Abel as we remember a beautiful mist at dawn.

25.

It's late: lightly wake the soul you put so heavily asleep.

26.

Even to say *you* presumes a little apophatic theology.

27.

The thief believes that his victim is guilty of something far worse.

28.

Snakes practice paraphs all day long.

29.

Clouds long to itch themselves on fields of nettles.

30.

There in the necks of bottles, the young.

31.

Each of us has a black thread hanging loose: pull it and you unravel.

32.

Americans think that Europe is Grandma's attic.

33.

Sin is addiction to self.

34.

Portraits of Victorian sages almost make us feel apologetic.

35.

Old houses sigh at night, just like their owners.

36.

Harpies were failed harpists: they learned to pick, not pluck.

37.

At night scissors do good imitations of crocodiles.

38.

Time evaporates like dew on a hot morning.

39.

Inside the mulberry, sharp angles of sunlight.

40.

Nouns wear adjectives to cover their nakedness.

41.

Theology is eloquent stuttering.

42.

When we wake we forget how to live.

43.

Sometimes the body thinks more quickly than the mind.

44.

Officer, that damn wind is beating up the Flag!

45.

The peals of the small bell run barefoot across the meadow.

46.

Chestnut voice, chaff words.

47.

A wise tongue seldom leaves its red palace.

48.

Summer: the heart chats up the mind.

49.

Idolatry is substance abuse.

50.

Poems are wells.

CRACKS

1.

Jesus, the gardener, weeds Eden.

2.

We hear; we seldom listen.

3.

Even big things get lost in the creases of time.

4.

Angels must be like red maples in Autumn.

5.

The real "dark lady" was the ink in Shakespeare's pen.

6.

To change your style, first change your life.

7.

At times we wish we could sit on our tongues.

8.

We hate cracks, but we always look through them.

9.

It's more difficult to love a man than to love humanity.

10.

We want the top leaf of a tree even if it's the same as the bottom leaf.

11.

Christian experience is not exposure to peril, it's avoiding it at the end.

12.

God did not come just as man; he also came as brother.

13.

Buck the system, sure, but it will buck you harder.

14.

One does not age, but one's friends sure do.

15.

If cats were diurnal, we would like them less.

16.

A garden should be loved before it is pruned.

17.

Our early errors are slightly alleviated by our teachers' deaths.

18.

We weep when slicing onions but not when cutting meat.

19.

Americans are poor readers because one can't read in a car.

20.

Like gannets, the saints dive into God.

21.

Universities seldom put out the trash.

22.

It takes three generations for someone to die.

23.

The passive voice welcomes evil.

24.

Goodness slips between grand ideas of goodness.

25.

When a deer walks the neighborhood, our tenure seems fragile.

26.

Trees always offer advice to clouds, but it's never taken.

27.

Medical science keeps us alive so that we might be bored for longer.

28.

Bad art dangles the world's skin before us, saying it's flesh and bone.

29.

When we weep in dreams, our waking eyes are wet.

30.

In the battle between love and death most people are onlookers.

31.

If you're not an extremist in *something*, what the hell are you?

32.

We skim sense from the world and leave its meaning.

33.

God lives in rhythm.

34.

Before long only the wealthy will be able to enjoy silence.

35.

One's middle name slyly hints at an alternate life one could lead.

36.

Politics is memory laced with will.

37.

The vices are mostly black, the virtues often gray.

38.

Compassion is a gateway to a mansion we seldom reach.

39.

"Liberty" is mostly soft soap sold by dirty politicians.

40.

The heart, also, needs vision correction.

41.

In philosophy too much proof can go to your head.

42.

Latin crystalizes the mind, Italian caramelizes it.

43.

Another Fall: from icons to iPhones.

44.

Modernity suppresses rhythm.

45.

Text messages are loquacious gnats.

46.

A place is where something has taken place.

47.

A cloud's on fire! No, it's only smoke.

48.

Life: a child walking into a dense forest.

49.

True knowledge is intimacy.

50.

Any road takes you into the dark.

CATCHES

1.

We remember sorrow more sharply than joy.

2.

Pride is inflammation of the soul.

3.

Good haiku taste like wasabi.

4.

The venetian blinds slice the fresh light.

5.

Awakening: the soul stretching.

6.

Reading the Bible is being a bit too close to a great fire.

7.

There, there, little sparrow, you play the xylophone beautifully!

8.

Gossip is doodling with others.

9.

It's no djinn — just steam from the artichokes!

10.

All tomatoes secretly long to be seraphs.

11.

The future beckons us, then looks away.

12.

In vino veritas — or perhaps a gnat.

13.

Hell is real: we visit several times before we die.

14.

Jokes fade when repeated, but less so than those who tell them.

15.

Confession turns circles into spirals.

16.

Some trees carve their names into our hearts.

17.

Meeting someone new is like standing on the edge of a cliff.

18.

Our vices grip us tightly.

19.

Our childhood memories are ruined houses.

20.

Always plant a few flowers in the mind.

21.

"Mystical experience": the sudden burning away of mist.

22.

Death can only squint at us.

23.

The grape skin of the moment almost bursts.

24.

The last page of a carnet is always cold.

25.

We do not come from monkeys, but we sure act like them.

26.

One thing American politics lacks is an extreme middle.

27.

Tourists visit a country but find only cities.

28.

I touch Grandfather's watch and I touch him.

29.

Good concepts outlast good arguments.

30.

The first yellow leaf — beauty, then fear.

31.

The gentle bury the brave.

32.

Seedless melons; classes without tests.

33.

Pessimism is smog that never lifts.

34.

We admire the complex and love the simple.

35.

It's better to be heard by God than overheard by him.

36.

Aphorisms should be written on garlic skin.

37.

Decisions come over one, like moods.

38.

Habit abridges beauty.

39.

Bad religion survives good philosophy.

40.

Some ideas produce allergic reactions.

41.

Whiskey sings the Blues.

42.

Life: go, undergo, go.

43.

Prayer is kneeling at attention.

44.

Memories are impatient; they interrupt us constantly.

45.

Night falls from within as well.

46.

Eros everywhere: the tangled weeds.

47.

Poems are catches.

48.

We get lost even within ourselves.

49.

Don't worry, you will be forgotten.

50.

When we love, we know.

ROOTS

1.

An elegy is written in her eyes.

2.

Flute music — bright clusters of grapes.

3.

We make our way to heaven like crippled snails.

4.

Water finds its level, justice doesn't.

5.

Somehow the alphabet gives us the cosmos.

6.

There are hands in which God rests.

7.

Promotion case: he doesn't publish but he smokes with style

8.

So patriotic, she makes toupées for bald eagles.

9.

Sometimes my name spreads its wings.

10.

Life is difficult: some people lodge above it, others beneath it.

11.

For some, the superfluous is simply not enough.

12.

Only humility prepares us for death.

13.

Just one set of footprints: a young beach.

14.

If it can't be shortened, it's not modern.

15.

Latin reflects light, Greek refracts it.

16.

Mirrors are the best critics.

17.

My future fits perfectly in my pen nib.

18.

We go to bed in the present, dream in the past, wake in the future.

19.

Kindness is so much rarer than love.

20.

Days are risks — or gambles.

21.

Creation does not encumber us: atoms are mostly empty.

22.

Perception is a tyrant.

23.

The ocean explodes on the beach and puts itself out.

24.

Inside, the night goes on forever.

25.

Aphorisms — espresso for the soul!

26.

The dead travel quickest in the early hours.

27.

The yellow brick road never ends.

28.

Our childhood toys turn into needles.

29.

Some jokes are baubles; others, daggers.

30.

Like everything else, doing nothing can be done well or badly.

31.

Sunlight dawdling in the mist . . .

32.

Exposed tree roots are the grammar of earth.

33.

When you read a book well, you polish it.

34.

We quest first for what we want, then for what we've lost.

35.

Your pupil, my most intimate of mirrors.

36.

Old mosquito nets reek of sweaty moonlight.

37.

The happy life always has one black thread hanging loose.

38.

You can sometimes taste dirt in Homer's lines.

39.

The Blues sounds older than the rain.

40.

We wait for what's already been.

41.

Those back roads are still fleeing from the city.

42.

When feverish, we see through things.

43.

Your library is your root system.

44.

Impatient, the old become ghosts before they die.

45.

Our bones are quiet; they know that they will win.

46.

Only cowards are always kind.

47.

One caress lights up the whole body.

48.

Dying, that dark aqueduct.

49.

Novelists keep diaries, philosophers don't.

50.

The quest for certainty goes through snickets, not fields.

TASTES

1.

Redwing parrots staggering beside the rotten mangoes.

2.

Each hour of summer plump with heat ...

3.

The kingdom is close — that old man sagging on a bench.

4.

Our childhood homes are haunted houses.

5.

Death's bony gaze at Surfer's on a summer day ...

6.

We do not need ambrosia if we have art.

7.

You want a bigger congregation? Try donuts after church.

8.

Few ideas fit the heart as well as the head.

9.

The living-room clock holds us all in siege.

10.

I do not own my pain; my pain owns me.

11.

Intelligence tastes too much like an apple.

12.

Blueberries lit by quiet August rain ...

13.

Good morning, moon. Hurry on now or you'll be late for dinner!

14.

Dragonflies are prototypes of angels.

15.

Sin is making eyes at death.

16.

Gobbling up the overripe days of summer ...

17.

Grandfather smokes my past in his pipe.

18.

Any rope can be a noose.

19.

How you regard the road makes you a pilgrim.

20.

A smile can also be a blade.

21.

Edgy people are always on the verge of something.

22.

Scissors beside the family album ...

23.

Rain is a rare species of breath.

24.

Her bare feet walk through my nights.

25.

When a leader excessively loves his nation, watch out!

26.

The rose thorns keep trying to snag the mist.

27.

Her last footprint on my path . . .

28.

The whippoorwill knows when I will die.

29.

Fear reminds us that we are animals.

30.

Lightning — as when an angel passes by too close.

31.

Emotions cross us and double-cross us, too.

32.

I touched her fifty years ago, and still I cannot leave her room.

33.

Only God calls me by my secret name.

34.

Too poor for the pictures, I watched the moon instead.

35.

My prayer is a firefly.

36.

One violin can beggar many hearts.

37.

A poem is a party — or a wake.

38.

In a vase, flowers are nude; in a garden, naked.

39.

If you skin the Autumn air, you'll hear the Blues.

40.

When there's no reason to hope, one begins to hope.

41.

To write one line, one must forget many books.

42.

The liar tastes his lie.

43.

Quests begin with questions.

44.

Poor philosophy now sits under a bonsai tree of life.

45.

The longest suspense bridge joins China and America.

46.

Dear thrush, I watch you build your nest so often that I almost live there too.

47.

My cat licks even where he's wet.

48.

When Jesus was alive, the sky for once felt small.

49.

Even when I pulled the thorn from my flesh it smelled of her.

50.

Sunburned pineapples dumped along a back road . . .

PINPRICKS

1.

Thinking with a carnet — the little way.

2.

Where hatred is, fear was.

3.

If the words rise up to meet you, it's poetry.

4.

Concepts step aside when love comes in.

5.

True authority disdains power.

6.

Sometimes we are tangents to ourselves.

7.

God produces us and prompts us but doesn't direct us.

8.

Art prunes our lives.

9.

Hot days are soft prisons.

10.

The lizard running up my leg cools me down.

11.

A windy Fall day: I walk outside and become a flag.

12.

Spring days do somersaults before we get up.

13.

Certain poems look at us the way icons do.

14.

A river of daisies runs through the field.

15.

You don't have to like the neighbor: love is quite enough.

16.

My Grandmother's China cups have no cracks; it's time that's cracked.

17.

We have the whole world and still we flirt with the void.

18.

One person looks at nature; another, at creation.

19.

Eating white grapes while watching raindrops on the window . . .

20.

Bad dreams bruise our brains.

21.

Smooth voices have hidden traps.

22.

The attic is the unconscious of the house.

23.

I leaned against the pear tree: and I blossomed.

24.

The day has lost its rudder.

25.

We make love; and only then eat figs with cream.

26.

I forgot my key: I can go anywhere.

27.

I walk into the field at dawn. I should have come here on my knees.

28.

I'm somewhere in the middle; both ends press on me.

29.

The truth is whole but mostly found in scraps.

30.

My father still looks at me from his coffin.

31.

We suspect some poems of being two-way mirrors.

32.

A hummingbird is made of haiku.

33.

A butterfly pauses on my glass of milk. And so life passes.

34.

Aphorisms are little birds, pecking, pecking . . .

35.

Poems remember more than they say.

36.

When you contemplate, time flows around you not through you.

37.

Modern cosmography is probably like Medieval cartography.

38.

Platonists need more paperweights than others.

39.

Only the greatest mathematicians are ever free in what they do.

40.

I dress myself entirely in jasmine: and then I wake.

41.

Leaves are maps of the forest.

42.

The ceiling fan is a UFO that's just about to land.

43.

The moral life isn't tidy but it *is* patterned.

44.

A bad teacher is a cage.

45.

Reading fertilizes books.

46.

Persons aren't natural but bodies are.

47.

Everything good was created by God; the rest, by committee.

48.

Fundamentalism is fast food.

49.

Death is a pinprick in the dark; we must all squeeze through.

50.

Horizons heal.

1974–2025

The Poiema Poetry Series

COLLECTIONS IN THIS SERIES INCLUDE:

Six Sundays Toward a Seventh by Sydney Lea
Epitaphs for the Journey by Paul Mariani
Within This Tree of Bones by Robert Siegel
Particular Scandals by Julie L. Moore
Gold by Barbara Crooker
A Word In My Mouth by Robert Cording
Say This Prayer into the Past by Paul Willis
Scape by Luci Shaw
Conspiracy of Light by D.S. Martin
Second Sky by Tania Runyan
Remembering Jesus by John Leax
What Cannot Be Fixed by Jill Pelaez Baumgaertner
Still Working It Out by Brad Davis
The Hatching of the Heart by Margo Swiss
Collage of Seoul by Jae Newman
Twisted Shapes of Light by William Jolliff
These Intricacies by David Harrity
Where the Sky Opens by Laurie Klein
True, False, None of the Above by Marjorie Maddox
The Turning Aside anthology edited by D.S. Martin
Falter by Marjorie Stelmach
Phases by Mischa Willett
Second Bloom by Anya Krugovoy Silver
Adam, Eve, & the Riders of the Apocalypse anthology edited by D.S. Martin
Your Twenty-First Century Prayer Life by Nathaniel Lee Hansen
Habitation of Wonder by Abigail Carroll
Ampersand by D.S. Martin
Full Worm Moon by Julie L. Moore
Ash & Embers by James A. Zoller
The Book of Kells by Barbara Crooker
Reaching Forever by Philip C. Kolin
The Book of Bearings by Diane Glancy

In a Strange Land anthology edited by D.S. Martin
What I Have I Offer With Two Hands by Jacob Stratman
Slender Warble by Susan Cowger
Madonna, Complex by Jen Stewart Fueston
No Reason by Jack Stewart
Abundance by Andrew Lansdown
Angelicus by D.S. Martin
Trespassing on the Mount of Olives by Brad Davis
The Angel of Absolute Zero by Marjorie Stelmach
Duress by Karen An-hwei Lee
Wolf Intervals by Graham Hillard
To Heaven's Rim anthology edited by Burl Horniachek
Cup My Days Like Water by Abigail Carroll
Soon Done with the Crosses by Claude Wilkinson
House of 49 Doors by Laurie Klein
Hawk and Songbird by Susan Cowger
Ponds by J.C. Scharl
The Farewell Suites by Andrew Lansdown
Let's Call It Home by Luke Harvey
Forbearance by Cameron Brooks